BACKYARD CHICKEN COOP IDEAS AND PLANS

Build Your Own Stylish, Secure and Practical Chicken Housing - Complete Blueprints and Step-by-Step Instructions for 30+ Coops and Runs to Fit Any Space

Graham F. Gardener

A Heartfelt Thank You

We extend our heartfelt gratitude to each and every one of you who has taken the time to delve into the world of backyard chicken keeping with us. Your curiosity, enthusiasm, and dedication to learning more about this topic have not gone unnoticed, and we are deeply thankful for your interest and engagement.

By exploring the intricacies of raising chickens in your own backyard, you have shown a commitment to fostering a deeper connection with nature and a desire to contribute positively to your community and the world around you. Whether you're a seasoned chicken keeper or someone just starting out on this journey, your willingness to learn and grow inspires us all.

We also want to express our gratitude to the chickens themselves, for the joy, companionship, and nourishment they bring into our lives. Their gentle clucks, playful antics, and delicious eggs remind us of the beauty and abundance of the natural world, and we are grateful for the opportunity to share our lives with these remarkable creatures.

As we reflect on the knowledge and insights shared in this guide, let us carry forward a sense of appreciation for the connections we have forged and the community we have built together. May we continue to learn from each other, support one another, and celebrate the joys of backyard chicken keeping for years to come.

With sincere thanks and warm wishes,

TABLE OF CONTENT

INTRODUCTION

In the heart of a bustling suburb, nestled among neatly manicured lawns and tidy flower beds, Bright's backyard was an oasis of greenery and life. Surrounded by the hum of everyday existence, he found solace in the simple pleasures of tending to his garden and nurturing his growing flock of chickens.

For Bright, the decision to raise chickens was not just about the promise of fresh eggs or the allure of self-sufficiency; it was a journey of connection—a connection to the land, to the rhythms of nature, and to the timeless traditions of generations past. But as he embarked on this new adventure, he quickly realized that building a quality coop was essential to the well-being of his feathered companions and the success of his backyard homestead.

Enter "Feathered Retreats: Inspiring Backyard Chicken Coop Ideas and Plans." From the moment Bright cracked open its pages, he knew he had stumbled upon a treasure trove of knowledge and inspiration. As he flipped through the vibrant photographs and detailed blueprints, he felt a sense of excitement building within him—a vision of the perfect coop taking shape in his mind's eye.

With each turn of the page, Bright found himself drawn deeper into the world of backyard chicken keeping. He marveled at the rustic charm of weathered barn wood and the sleek elegance of modern designs. He imagined his own coop nestled amidst the lush greenery of his garden, a sanctuary where his chickens could roost in comfort and style.

But "Feathered Retreats" offered more than just design inspiration; it was a comprehensive guide to every aspect of coop construction and maintenance. From sizing specifications to protective enclosures, nesting boxes to ventilation needs, Bright found all the information he needed to create a safe and nurturing environment for his flock.

And as he reached the end of the introduction, Bright couldn't help but feel a sense of anticipation for the journey ahead. Keeping a small flock of chickens in his backyard was more than just a hobby—it was an enriching experience that connected him to nature's food cycle and brought joy to his everyday life.

Keeping a small flock of chickens in your backyard is an enriching experience that delivers a bounty of fresh eggs and connects you with nature's food cycle. The growing "backyard chicken" movement has captured imaginations in both urban and suburban neighborhoods across the country. But getting started with a quality coop is essential.

Embracing the Joys of Backyard Chicken Keeping

There's something truly special about stepping into the world of backyard chicken keeping. It's not just about raising birds for eggs or meat—it's about embracing a lifestyle that connects us deeply to the rhythms of nature and the simple joys of everyday life.

For many of us, the decision to keep chickens in our backyard isn't made lightly. It's a choice rooted in a desire for connection—to the land, to our food, and to the creatures that share our world. As we welcome these feathered friends into our lives, we open our hearts to a new chapter filled with wonder, laughter, and a profound sense of fulfillment.

There's a magic in waking up to the gentle clucking of hens as they greet the morning sun, their soft feathers illuminated by its golden rays. There's a sense of pride that swells within us as we gather fresh eggs from the nesting boxes, each one a testament to the care and love we've poured into our flock. And there's a deep sense of satisfaction that comes from knowing that we're providing our families with food that is not only nutritious but also ethically and sustainably sourced.

But perhaps most importantly, there's a bond that forms between us and our chickens—a bond that transcends words and fills our hearts with warmth and joy. As we spend time in their company, we come to know each bird as a unique individual, with her own quirks, preferences, and personality traits. We learn to listen to their gentle clucks and watch for the subtle cues that reveal their needs and desires.

In a world that often feels chaotic and disconnected, backyard chicken keeping offers us a refuge—a sanctuary where we can slow down, breathe deeply, and reconnect with the simple pleasures of life. It's a reminder that amidst the hustle and bustle of modern living, there is beauty to be found in the small moments—the soft flutter of wings, the warmth of a freshly laid egg, the quiet contentment of a flock at rest.

So let us embrace the joys of backyard chicken keeping with open arms and open hearts. Let us revel in the beauty of nature's bounty and the timeless rhythms of the farmyard. And let us cherish each day spent in the company of our feathered companions, knowing that in their presence, we find peace, purpose, and a profound sense of belonging.

Chapter 1: Rustic Charm

Embracing the Beauty of Nature

There's a certain magic that comes with immersing oneself in the beauty of nature, a magic that touches the soul and stirs the heart in profound ways. In the world of backyard chicken keeping, this magic is palpable—a reminder of the awe-inspiring wonder that surrounds us each and every day.

As we step outside and breathe in the fresh, crisp air of the morning, we are greeted by a symphony of sounds—the gentle rustle of leaves, the melodious chirping of birds, the rhythmic babbling of a nearby stream. In these moments, we are reminded of the interconnectedness of all living things, of the intricate dance of life that unfolds in every corner of the natural world.

But it's not just the sights and sounds of nature that captivate us—it's the feeling of being truly alive, of being part of something greater than ourselves. As we watch our chickens peck and scratch in the earth, their vibrant plumage shimmering in the sunlight, we are reminded of the resilience and beauty of the natural world.

There's a sense of wonder that comes from witnessing the cycle of life firsthand—from the delicate emergence of a chick from its shell to the proud strut of a rooster as he surveys his domain. In these moments, we are humbled by the majesty of creation and inspired to cherish and protect the fragile ecosystems that sustain us all.

But perhaps most of all, there's a deep sense of peace that settles over us as we lose ourselves in the embrace of nature. In the quiet solitude of the backyard, surrounded by the beauty of blooming flowers and lush greenery, we find solace and renewal. It's here, in this sacred space, that we are able to reconnect with ourselves and with the natural world, to find clarity and perspective in a world that often feels chaotic and overwhelming.

So let us embrace the beauty of nature with open arms and open hearts. Let us revel in the simple joys of watching a butterfly alight on a flower, of feeling the warmth of the sun on our skin, of listening to the gentle rhythm of the earth. And let us remember that in embracing the beauty of nature, we are also embracing a part of ourselves—a part that is wild, untamed, and endlessly resilient.

Incorporating Reclaimed Materials

There's a certain allure to breathing new life into old treasures, to transforming forgotten relics into cherished works of art. It's a journey of creativity, ingenuity, and connection—one that speaks to the soul and resonates with the rhythms of the earth.

When it comes to building a backyard chicken coop, the possibilities are endless. But for those who are drawn to the rustic charm of days gone by, there's something truly special about incorporating reclaimed materials into the design.

There's a sense of nostalgia that comes from working with reclaimed wood—each weathered board telling a story of days gone by, of hard work and perseverance, of a simpler way of life. As we carefully select each piece, running our fingers over the rough-hewn surface, we can't help but feel a sense of reverence for the craftsmanship of generations past.

But it's not just the history imbued in these materials that captivates us—it's the beauty of imperfection, the way that time and weather have left their mark, adding character and depth to every knot and grain. In a world that often prizes uniformity and perfection, there's something profoundly refreshing about embracing the natural patina of aged wood, the rich hues of weathered metal, the delicate intricacies of vintage hardware.

As we set to work, sawing and hammering, shaping and sanding, we find ourselves transported to another time and place—a time when things were built to last, when craftsmanship was valued above all else. And as our coop begins to take shape, we can't help but feel a sense of pride in knowing that we've created something truly unique, something that speaks to our values and our love of the land.

But perhaps most importantly, there's a sense of connection that comes from working with reclaimed materials—a connection to the earth, to our ancestors, and to the countless generations that will come after us. In a world that often feels disconnected and fragmented, there's something profoundly comforting about knowing that we are part of a larger story, a story that spans centuries and spans continents, a story that binds us all together inextricably.

So let us embrace the beauty of reclaimed materials with open arms and open hearts. Let us revel in the history and heritage that they represent, and let us honor the craftsmanship and ingenuity of those who came before us. And as we build our backyard chicken coops, let us remember that we are not just creating shelters for our feathered friends—we are creating legacies, stories, and connections that will endure for generations to come.

Creating Cozy Cottage Retreats

There's a certain charm to the quaint simplicity of a cottage nestled amidst a garden teeming with life—a charm that speaks to the soul and invites us to slow down, breathe deeply, and savor the beauty of everyday moments. It's a feeling of warmth and comfort, of nostalgia for a bygone era, and of longing for a simpler way of life.

When it comes to building a backyard chicken coop, there's no design quite as inviting as the cozy cottage retreat. With its pitched roof and charming details, it evokes images of storybook cottages tucked away in the English countryside, surrounded by fields of wildflowers and grazing sheep.

But it's not just the aesthetic appeal of the cottage retreat that captivates us—it's the feeling of home that it embodies. As we set to work, hammering and sawing, painting and decorating, we find ourselves transported to a world where time moves a little slower, where laughter echoes through sun-dappled meadows, and where the scent of freshly baked bread wafts through the air.

There's a sense of satisfaction that comes from knowing that we are creating a sanctuary for our feathered friends—a place where they can roost in comfort and safety, protected from the elements and free to wander among the flowers and herbs. As we add finishing touches like flower boxes and picket fences, we can't help but feel a sense of pride in knowing that we've created something truly special, something that brings joy and beauty to our backyard.

But perhaps most importantly, there's a sense of connection that comes from building a cozy cottage retreat—a connection to the land, to our heritage, and to the rhythms of nature. In a world that often feels hectic and disconnected, there's something profoundly comforting about knowing that we are part of a larger tapestry, woven together by threads of love, creativity, and the timeless beauty of the natural world.

So let us embrace the cozy cottage retreat with open arms and open hearts. Let us revel in the warmth and charm that it brings to our backyard, and let us cherish the memories that we create within its walls. And as we gather around its hearth on chilly evenings, surrounded by the laughter of loved ones and the gentle clucking of our feathered companions, let us give thanks for the simple joys that make life truly beautiful.

Designing Barn-Inspired Masterpieces

There's a certain grandeur to the iconic silhouette of a barn standing tall against the horizon—a symbol of hard work, resilience, and the enduring beauty of rural life. It's a sight that stirs something deep within us, evoking feelings of awe and admiration for the craftsmanship of generations past and the timeless allure of rustic charm.

When it comes to building a backyard chicken coop, drawing inspiration from the humble barn can transform a simple structure into a masterpiece of design and functionality. With its sturdy beams, steeply pitched roof, and classic red siding, the barn-inspired coop captures the essence of country living, inviting us to embrace the simplicity and elegance of rural architecture.

But it's not just the exterior of the barn-inspired coop that captivates us—it's the sense of history and tradition that it embodies. As we carefully select materials and plan out every detail, we find ourselves drawn into a world where hard work and craftsmanship are valued above all else, where each beam and board tells a story of days gone by.

There's a sense of pride that comes from knowing that we are carrying on a legacy—a legacy of stewardship and respect for the land, of self-sufficiency and resilience in the face of adversity. As we raise the walls and raise the roof, we can't help but feel a sense of connection to the farmers and homesteaders who came before us, who built their lives with their own two hands and passed down their knowledge from one generation to the next.

But perhaps most importantly, there's a sense of wonder that comes from seeing our vision take shape before our eyes—a vision of a barn-inspired masterpiece that blends seamlessly with the landscape, providing a safe and comfortable home for our feathered friends. As we put the finishing touches on our coop, adding touches like sliding barn doors and rustic accents, we can't help but feel a sense of satisfaction in knowing that we've created something truly special, something that honors the spirit of the barn while embracing the joys of backyard chicken keeping.

So let us embrace the beauty of barn-inspired design with open arms and open hearts. Let us revel in the timeless appeal of rural architecture, and let us cherish the memories that we create within the walls of our masterpiece. And as we stand back and admire our handiwork, surrounded by the sounds of clucking hens and rustling leaves, let us give thanks for the opportunity to connect with nature and with each other in a meaningful and profound way.

Chapter 2: Modern Marvels

Infusing Sleek Style Into Backyard Spaces

There's a certain allure to the sleek and modern aesthetic—a harmonious blend of clean lines, minimalist design, and contemporary elegance that speaks to our desire for simplicity and sophistication. In the world of backyard chicken keeping, infusing sleek style into our outdoor spaces offers a fresh perspective—a way to marry form and function in perfect harmony.

When it comes to designing a modern backyard chicken coop, the possibilities are endless. From sleek, geometric shapes to minimalist color palettes, there are countless ways to infuse a touch of contemporary flair into our outdoor spaces. Whether nestled amidst a bustling urban landscape or set against the backdrop of a sprawling suburban garden, a modern coop adds a touch of sophistication to any backyard.

But it's not just about aesthetics—infusing sleek style into our backyard spaces is also about creating environments that are as functional as they are fashionable. As we carefully plan out every detail, from the layout of the coop to the choice of materials, we find ourselves drawn to designs that prioritize efficiency, convenience, and ease of maintenance.

There's a sense of satisfaction that comes from knowing that we've created a space that not only looks good but also works hard for us and our feathered friends. From automated feeders and waterers to solar-powered lighting and ventilation systems, a modern coop is a testament to the power of innovation and technology in the pursuit of sustainable living.

But perhaps most importantly, infusing sleek style into our backyard spaces is about embracing the future—a future where beauty and functionality go hand in hand, where design is driven by a desire to create spaces that enhance our lives and connect us to the world around us. As we stand back and admire our modern masterpiece, surrounded by the sounds of contented clucks and the gentle rustle of leaves, we can't help but feel a sense of pride in knowing that we've created a space that is as stylish as it is sustainable.

So let us embrace the sleek style of modern design with open arms and open hearts. Let us revel in the beauty of clean lines and minimalist aesthetics, and let us celebrate the ingenuity and creativity that make our backyard spaces truly special. And as we enjoy the fruits of our labor, surrounded by the beauty of nature and the warmth of our feathered companions, let us give thanks for the opportunity to create spaces that bring joy and inspiration to our lives each and every day.

Exploring Innovative Materials and Designs

There's a sense of excitement that comes from pushing the boundaries of creativity, from stepping outside the box and exploring new possibilities. In the realm of backyard chicken coops, this sense of adventure manifests itself in the form of innovative materials and designs—a world of endless potential waiting to be discovered.

As we embark on this journey of exploration, we find ourselves drawn to materials that challenge our preconceptions and ignite our imagination. From sustainable bamboo and recycled plastics to cutting-edge composite materials, there's a wealth of options available to us, each with its own unique qualities and characteristics.

But it's not just about the materials themselves—it's about the stories they tell, the connections they forge, and the impact they have on our lives and the world around us. As we delve into the world of innovative design, we find ourselves inspired by the ingenuity and creativity of those who dare to think differently, to question the status quo, and to push the boundaries of what is possible.

There's a sense of wonder that comes from seeing these materials come to life in our backyard spaces, from watching as they transform into sleek, modern coops that blend seamlessly with the landscape.

From translucent panels that bathe our coops in natural light to modular systems that allow for endless customization, innovative materials and designs offer us a glimpse into a future where sustainability and beauty coexist.

But perhaps most importantly, exploring innovative materials and designs is about embracing the spirit of adventure, of daring to dream big and chase after our wildest aspirations. It's about recognizing that the world is full of possibilities waiting to be explored, and that the only limits are the ones we place on ourselves.

So let us embrace the thrill of discovery with open arms and open hearts. Let us revel in the beauty of innovative materials and designs, and let us celebrate the ingenuity and creativity that make our backyard spaces truly special. And as we embark on this journey of exploration, surrounded by the beauty of nature and the warmth of our feathered companions, let us remember that the sky is the limit—and that the best is yet to come.

Incorporating Minimalist Aesthetics

There's a certain serenity that comes from stripping away the excess, from embracing simplicity and clarity in all aspects of life. In the world of backyard chicken coops, incorporating minimalist aesthetics is not just about design—it's about creating spaces that inspire calm, evoke beauty, and celebrate the essence of what truly matters.

As we embark on the journey of incorporating minimalist aesthetics into our backyard spaces, we find ourselves drawn to clean lines, uncluttered spaces, and a sense of openness that invites us to breathe deeply and savor the moment. It's a feeling of liberation, of letting go of the unnecessary and embracing the essential.

But it's not just about aesthetics—it's about mindset. It's about recognizing that true beauty lies not in the accumulation of things, but in the appreciation of what we already have. As we pare back the layers and simplify our surroundings, we find ourselves connecting more deeply with the natural world, with our feathered companions, and with ourselves.

There's a sense of peace that comes from living with less, from surrounding ourselves with objects that bring us joy and meaning. In a world that often feels overwhelming and chaotic, incorporating minimalist aesthetics into our backyard spaces offers us a refuge—a sanctuary where we can find solace and renewal amidst the hustle and bustle of everyday life.

But perhaps most importantly, incorporating minimalist aesthetics is about honoring the beauty of simplicity, of recognizing that less is often more, and that true luxury lies not in extravagance, but in elegance and restraint. It's about embracing a lifestyle that is mindful, intentional, and deeply fulfilling—a lifestyle that allows us to focus on what truly matters and let go of the rest.

So let us embrace the beauty of minimalist aesthetics with open arms and open hearts. Let us revel in the simplicity and clarity that they bring to our backyard spaces, and let us celebrate the joy and freedom that come from living with less. And as we cultivate spaces that inspire peace, beauty, and connection, let us remember that true abundance lies not in the things we possess, but in the moments we share and the love we give.

Balancing Form and Functionality

There's a delicate dance that takes place when designing any space—a dance between form and functionality, between beauty and practicality. In the world of backyard chicken coops, this dance is especially important, as we strive to create spaces that are not only aesthetically pleasing but also serve the needs of our feathered friends and ourselves.

As we set out to balance form and functionality in our backyard spaces, we find ourselves faced with countless decisions—each one a delicate balancing act between style and substance. Do we prioritize sleek lines and modern design, or do we opt for sturdy construction and ample space? Do we choose materials that are beautiful but fragile, or do we prioritize durability and longevity?

It's a question that requires careful consideration, as we weigh the desire for beauty against the need for practicality. But ultimately, it's a question that can only be answered by listening to our hearts and trusting our instincts.

There's a sense of satisfaction that comes from finding the perfect balance between form and functionality—a feeling of accomplishment that comes from creating spaces that are not only visually stunning but also highly functional. It's a feeling of harmony, of knowing that every decision we make contributes to the overall success of our design.

But it's not just about creating spaces that look good—it's about creating spaces that feel good, that resonate with our hearts and souls on a deeper level. As we stand back and admire our handiwork, surrounded by the beauty of nature and the warmth of our feathered companions, we can't help but feel a sense of pride in knowing that we've created something truly special, something that brings joy and inspiration to our lives each and every day.

So let us embrace the challenge of balancing form and functionality with open arms and open hearts. Let us revel in the creative process, trusting that with patience and perseverance, we can create spaces that are both beautiful and practical. And let us celebrate the joy and fulfillment that come from finding harmony in the spaces we inhabit, knowing that when form and functionality come together in perfect balance, magic happens.

Chapter 3: Space-Saving Solutions

Maximizing Urban Environments

In the hustle and bustle of city life, finding space for backyard chicken keeping can feel like a daunting challenge. But for those of us who call the urban jungle home, the rewards of creating a small oasis of greenery and life amidst the concrete and steel are immeasurable.

As we set out to maximize urban environments for backyard chicken keeping, we are met with a unique set of opportunities and constraints. Space is at a premium, and every square inch must be carefully considered and utilized to its fullest potential. But with creativity and ingenuity, we discover that even the smallest of spaces can be transformed into thriving havens for our feathered friends.

There's a sense of excitement that comes from turning overlooked corners and forgotten alleyways into vibrant urban gardens, teeming with life and possibility. It's a feeling of empowerment, of reclaiming our connection to the land and the food we eat, even in the midst of the city's hustle and bustle.

But it's not just about creating spaces for chickens to roost—it's about creating spaces for us to connect with nature and with each other. As we tend to our urban gardens and watch our chickens scratch and peck in the earth, we find ourselves slowing down, breathing deeply, and savoring the simple joys of life.

There's a sense of community that comes from sharing our urban spaces with others, from inviting neighbors to join us in the joy of backyard chicken keeping and the satisfaction of growing our own food. It's a feeling of camaraderie, of knowing that we are part of something bigger than ourselves, something that brings us together and strengthens the bonds of friendship and community.

But perhaps most importantly, maximizing urban environments for backyard chicken keeping is about hope—for a future where cities are not just concrete jungles, but thriving ecosystems where people and nature coexist in harmony. It's a vision of a greener, more sustainable world, where even the smallest of actions can have a ripple effect that transforms our communities and our planet for the better.

So let us embrace the challenge of maximizing urban environments for backyard chicken keeping with open arms and open hearts. Let us revel in the beauty of green spaces amidst the concrete, and let us celebrate the resilience and resourcefulness of city dwellers who refuse to let the constraints of urban life hold them back. And as we watch our urban gardens grow and our chickens flourish, let us be reminded that even in the midst of the city's hustle and bustle, there is always room for beauty, for growth, and for connection.

Exploring Vertical Coop Designs

In the ever-evolving world of backyard chicken keeping, there's a sense of adventure that comes from exploring new horizons, from pushing the boundaries of what's possible. And when it comes to coop designs, few innovations are as exciting—or as space-saving—as the exploration of verticality.

As we set out to explore vertical coop designs, we're met with a sense of wonder and anticipation, like embarking on a journey to uncharted territories. The very notion of building upwards, rather than outwards, opens up a world of possibilities, allowing us to make the most of limited space while still providing a comfortable and safe environment for our feathered friends.

There's a sense of ingenuity that comes from thinking outside the box, from finding creative solutions to the challenges posed by urban living. With vertical coop designs, we're able to reclaim precious square footage in our backyard spaces, transforming even the smallest of plots into thriving havens for our chickens.

But it's not just about practicality—it's about the joy of discovery, of seeing our ideas take shape and come to life before our eyes. As we sketch out plans and gather materials, we can't help but feel a sense of excitement building within us, knowing that we're embarking on a journey that will not only benefit our chickens but also enrich our own lives in ways we never imagined.

There's a sense of satisfaction that comes from watching our vertical coop designs come together, from seeing our chickens explore their new home with curiosity and delight. It's a feeling of pride, of knowing that we've created something truly special, something that combines form and function in perfect harmony.

But perhaps most importantly, exploring vertical coop designs is about embracing innovation and embracing change, even in the face of uncertainty. It's about recognizing that the world is constantly evolving, and that by embracing new ideas and new technologies, we can create a brighter future for ourselves and for generations to come.

So let us embrace the challenge of exploring vertical coop designs with open arms and open hearts. Let us revel in the joy of discovery, and let us celebrate the spirit of ingenuity and creativity that drives us forward. And as we watch our vertical coops rise towards the sky, let us be reminded that the sky is the limit—and that with a little imagination and a lot of determination, anything is possible.

Creating Compact Coop-and-Run Combos

There's a sense of ingenuity that comes from finding clever solutions to space constraints, from making the most of every square inch of our backyard spaces. And when it comes to creating compact coop-and-run combos, this ingenuity is on full display, as we strive to provide our feathered friends with a safe and comfortable home while maximizing our limited outdoor space.

As we set out to create compact coop-and-run combos, we're met with a sense of determination and resourcefulness, like pioneers charting a course through uncharted territory. The challenge of fitting everything our chickens need—shelter, roosting space, nesting boxes, and outdoor run—into a compact footprint pushes us to think creatively and problem-solve like never before.

There's a sense of satisfaction that comes from seeing our vision come to life, from watching as our compact coop-and-run combos take shape before our eyes. With each nail hammered and each board secured, we feel a sense of pride knowing that we're providing our chickens with a cozy home that meets all their needs, even in the smallest of spaces.

But it's not just about functionality—it's about creating a space that feels like home, both for our chickens and for ourselves. As we add finishing touches like colorful paint, decorative trim, and cozy bedding, we can't help but feel a sense of warmth and happiness knowing that we're creating a space where both humans and chickens can thrive.

There's a sense of connection that comes from working together to create something special, from collaborating with family and friends to bring our vision to life. As we share ideas and lend a helping hand, we strengthen our bonds and create memories that will last a lifetime.

But perhaps most importantly, creating compact coop-and-run combos is about love—for our chickens, for the earth, and for each other. It's about recognizing that even in the smallest of spaces, there is room for growth, for beauty, and for connection. And as we watch our chickens explore their new home with joy and excitement, we're reminded that sometimes, the best things come in small packages.

So let us embrace the challenge of creating compact coop-and-run combos with open arms and open hearts. Let us revel in the joy of creativity, and let us celebrate the power of ingenuity and resourcefulness to transform our backyard spaces into havens of happiness and harmony. And as we gather around our compact coop-and-run combos, surrounded by the sounds of contented clucks and rustling leaves, let us give thanks for the opportunity to create spaces that bring joy and beauty to our lives each and every day.

Designing Rooftop Gardens

There's a certain magic that comes from transforming an urban rooftop into a lush oasis of greenery—a magic that speaks to our longing for connection with nature in the midst of the concrete jungle. As we set out to design rooftop gardens, we're filled with a sense of excitement and possibility, like explorers embarking on a journey to discover hidden treasures.

There's a sense of wonder that comes from seeing a barren rooftop come to life with vibrant plants, blooming flowers, and bustling wildlife. With each plant carefully selected and each garden bed meticulously arranged, we're able to create a sanctuary in the sky—a place where we can escape the noise and chaos of the city below and immerse ourselves in the beauty of the natural world.

But it's not just about creating a beautiful space—it's about creating a haven for ourselves and for the creatures that share our urban landscape. As we plant flowers to attract pollinators, install bird feeders to nourish our feathered friends, and set up bee hives to support local ecosystems, we're reminded of our interconnectedness with all living things.

There's a sense of peace that comes from tending to our rooftop gardens, from feeling the soil between our fingers and the sun on our faces. In the midst of the hustle and bustle of city life, our gardens offer us a refuge—a place where we can slow down, breathe deeply, and reconnect with the rhythms of the earth.

But perhaps most importantly, designing rooftop gardens is about hope—for a future where cities are not just concrete jungles, but vibrant, thriving ecosystems where humans and nature coexist in harmony. It's a vision of a greener, more sustainable world, where even the smallest green spaces can have a big impact on our lives and our planet.

So let us embrace the challenge of designing rooftop gardens with open hearts and open minds. Let us revel in the joy of creating spaces that bring beauty and life to our urban landscapes, and let us celebrate the power of nature to inspire, heal, and connect us all. And as we watch our rooftop gardens grow and flourish, let us be reminded that even in the heart of the city, there is always room for beauty, for growth, and for hope.

Chapter 4: DIY Delights

Unleashing Your Inner DIY Enthusiast

There's a fire that ignites within us when we embark on a do-it-yourself project—a spark of creativity, a surge of excitement, and a sense of empowerment that comes from taking matters into our own hands. As we unleash our inner DIY enthusiast, we're filled with a mix of anticipation and determination, like pioneers setting out to conquer uncharted territory.

There's a thrill that comes from diving into a DIY project, from rolling up our sleeves and getting our hands dirty. Whether it's building a chicken coop from scratch, creating a vertical garden, or crafting handmade decor for our outdoor space, every hammer swing and paintbrush stroke fills us with a sense of accomplishment and pride.

But it's not just about the end result—it's about the journey, the process of learning and growing along the way. As we tackle new challenges and overcome obstacles, we discover skills we never knew we had and unlock hidden talents waiting to be unleashed.

There's a sense of joy that comes from working with our hands, from breathing life into raw materials and watching our vision come to life before our eyes. With each cut of the saw and each stroke of the brush, we infuse a piece of ourselves into our projects, leaving behind a legacy of creativity and ingenuity.

But perhaps most importantly, unleashing our inner DIY enthusiast is about reclaiming our sense of agency, of realizing that we have the power to shape our surroundings and create the world we want to live in. In a world that often feels chaotic and uncertain, DIY projects offer us a sense of control—a way to make our mark and leave a lasting impact on the world around us.

So let us embrace the challenge of unleashing our inner DIY enthusiast with open arms and open hearts. Let us revel in the joy of creation, and let us celebrate the beauty of handmade craftsmanship in all its forms. And as we embark on this journey of self-discovery and creativity, let us be reminded that with passion, perseverance, and a little bit of elbow grease, anything is possible.

Building Basic A-Frame Structures

There's a certain charm to the simplicity of an A-frame structure—a timeless design that evokes images of cozy cabins nestled amidst towering pines and snow-capped peaks. As we set out to build basic A-frame structures, we're filled with a sense of nostalgia and adventure, like explorers venturing into the wilderness to build our own piece of paradise.

There's a satisfaction that comes from working with our hands, from shaping raw materials into something beautiful and functional. With each cut of the wood and each swing of the hammer, we feel a sense of connection to the earth and to the generations of craftsmen who came before us.

But it's not just about the physical act of building—it's about the journey of transformation, of turning a vision into reality. As we watch our A-frame structures take shape before our eyes, we're filled with a sense of wonder and awe, marveling at the beauty of our creation and the power of human ingenuity.

There's a sense of pride that comes from knowing that we've built something with our own two hands, something that will stand as a testament to our skill and perseverance for years to come. Whether it's a simple chicken coop or a rustic garden shed, our A-frame structures are more than just buildings—they're symbols of our ability to create, to innovate, and to leave our mark on the world.

But perhaps most importantly, building basic A-frame structures is about creating spaces that bring us closer to nature, that allow us to escape the hustle and bustle of everyday life and reconnect with the rhythms of the earth. Whether we're using our structures to house chickens, store gardening tools, or simply as a quiet retreat, they offer us a sanctuary—a place where we can find peace, solace, I find motivation in the natural world's splendor.

So let us embrace the challenge of building basic A-frame structures with open arms and open hearts. Let us revel in the joy of creation, and let us celebrate the timeless appeal of simple, elegant design. And as we stand back and admire our handiwork, surrounded by the beauty of our A-frame structures and the serenity of nature, let us be reminded that sometimes, the simplest things are also the most profound.

Customizing Coop Plans to Suit Your Needs

There's a special kind of excitement that comes from taking a standard blueprint and making it your own—a feeling of empowerment, creativity, and anticipation that fills the air as you set out to customize your coop plans. It's a journey that's deeply personal, as you tailor every detail to fit the unique needs of your flock and your space.

As you embark on the process of customizing coop plans, you're met with a sense of possibility and potential, like an artist faced with a blank canvas waiting to be transformed into a masterpiece. Every decision—from the size and layout of the coop to the materials and finishes—feels like a brushstroke on the canvas of your backyard, each one contributing to the overall beauty and functionality of your design.

But it's not just about aesthetics—it's about creating a space that reflects your values, your personality, and your vision for your backyard. Whether you're adding extra windows for more natural light, incorporating eco-friendly features like rainwater collection systems, or designing custom-built nesting boxes to accommodate your flock's specific needs, every choice you make is a reflection of who you are and what you care about.

There's a sense of pride that comes from seeing your customized coop plans come to life, from watching as your vision takes shape and becomes a reality before your eyes. With each nail hammered and each board cut to size, you feel a deep sense of satisfaction knowing that you've created something truly unique and special—a home for your chickens that is as one-of-a-kind as they are.

But perhaps most importantly, customizing coop plans is about creating a space that nurtures and supports your flock, providing them with everything they need to thrive and flourish. As you put the finishing touches on your design and open the doors to your newly customized coop, you feel a swell of emotion knowing that you've created a safe, comfortable, and loving home for your feathered friends.

So let us embrace the challenge of customizing coop plans with open arms and open hearts. Let us revel in the joy of creation, and let us celebrate the power of customization to transform a simple structure into a space that is uniquely our own. And as we stand back and admire our handiwork, surrounded by the sounds of contented clucks and the beauty of our backyard, let us be reminded that when we put our hearts into something, the results are truly magical.

Mastering Construction Techniques

There's a sense of craftsmanship that comes from mastering construction techniques—a feeling of pride, skill, and accomplishment that accompanies every nail driven and every joint secured. Whether you're a seasoned builder or a novice DIY enthusiast, the journey of mastering construction techniques is a rewarding one, filled with challenges and triumphs along the way.

As you delve into the world of construction, you're met with a sense of curiosity and wonder, like a student eager to soak up knowledge from a master craftsman. From learning the basics of measuring and cutting to mastering more advanced techniques like framing, roofing, and finishing, every lesson is an opportunity to expand your skills and deepen your understanding of the craft.

But it's not just about the technical aspects of construction—it's about developing a mindset of precision, patience, and attention to detail. As you hone your skills and refine your techniques, you begin to see the world through a different lens, noticing the subtle nuances of form and structure in everything around you.

There's a sense of satisfaction that comes from seeing your hard work come to fruition, from watching as a pile of raw materials transforms into a sturdy, functional structure. With each project completed, you gain confidence in your abilities and a sense of pride in your craftsmanship, knowing that you have the skills and knowledge to tackle even the most challenging of builds.

But perhaps most importantly, mastering construction techniques is about more than just building structures—it's about building dreams. Whether you're constructing a chicken coop, a garden shed, or your own dream home, the skills you acquire along the way empower you to bring your vision to life and design an area that is exclusively yours.

So let us embrace the challenge of mastering construction techniques with open arms and open hearts. Let us revel in the joy of learning, and let us celebrate the artistry and craftsmanship that make every project a work of art. And as we continue on our journey of discovery and growth, let us be reminded that with dedication, practice, and a willingness to learn, anything is possible.

Chapter 5: Functional Features

Prioritizing Health, Safety, and Comfort

In the realm of backyard chicken keeping, there's a fundamental principle that guides every decision we make: the well-being of our feathered friends always comes first. As we prioritize health, safety, and comfort in the care of our flock, we're driven by a deep sense of responsibility and compassion, knowing that the lives and happiness of our chickens depend on us.

Health is paramount in the world of chicken keeping, and we spare no effort in ensuring that our feathered companions are happy and thriving. From providing a balanced diet rich in nutrients to implementing regular health checks and vaccinations, we take proactive measures to safeguard the health of our flock and prevent the spread of disease.

Safety is another top priority, as we strive to create an environment that is free from hazards and dangers. We meticulously inspect our coops and runs, reinforcing weak spots and fortifying defenses against predators. From sturdy fencing to secure locks and latches, we leave no stone unturned in our quest to keep our chickens safe from harm.

But it's not just about physical safety—it's also about emotional well-being and comfort. We create cozy nesting boxes lined with soft bedding, providing a warm and inviting space for our hens to lay their eggs. We ensure ample ventilation and airflow in our coops, preventing overheating in the summer and maintaining warmth in the winter. And we take the time to observe and understand the behavior of our chickens, responding to their needs and preferences with empathy and care.

There's a sense of fulfillment that comes from knowing that we've created a space where our chickens can thrive, where they can live out their days in peace and contentment. With each cluck and each flap of their wings, we're reminded of the bond we share with these remarkable creatures, and the joy they bring to our lives.

But perhaps most importantly, prioritizing health, safety, and comfort is about more than just caring for our chickens—it's about stewardship, and the profound responsibility we have to protect and nurture the natural world around us. As we tend to our flock with love and dedication, we're reminded of the interconnectedness of all living things, and the importance of living in harmony with the earth and its creatures.

So let us continue to prioritize health, safety, and comfort in the care of our chickens, with open hearts and a steadfast commitment to their well-being. And as we watch them scratch and peck in the sun, surrounded by the beauty of nature and the warmth of our care, let us be reminded of the profound privilege it is to be their guardians and friends.

Implementing Effective Ventilation Systems

In the realm of backyard chicken coops, ensuring proper ventilation is crucial for the health and well-being of our feathered friends. As we set out to implement effective ventilation systems, we're driven by a deep understanding of the importance of fresh air and airflow in maintaining optimal conditions within the coop.

Ventilation plays a vital role in regulating temperature, removing excess moisture, and preventing the buildup of harmful gases like ammonia. Without adequate ventilation, coops can become hot and stuffy in the summer, leading to heat stress and respiratory issues for chickens. In the winter, poor ventilation can trap moisture inside the coop, increasing the risk of frostbite and respiratory infections.

To implement effective ventilation systems, we carefully consider the layout and design of our coops, ensuring that there are ample openings for air to flow freely. This may include windows, vents, and eave openings strategically positioned to promote cross-ventilation and natural airflow. We also install hardware cloth or mesh screens over openings to keep out predators while allowing air to circulate.

But it's not just about passive ventilation—active ventilation systems like fans and exhaust vents can also play a crucial role in maintaining optimal air quality within the coop. By installing exhaust fans or solar-powered vents, we can quickly remove stale air and moisture, ensuring that our chickens have access to fresh, clean air at all times.

There's a sense of peace that comes from knowing that we've created a comfortable and healthy environment for our chickens to thrive. With each breath of fresh air that fills the coop, we're reminded of the importance of proper ventilation in promoting the health and well-being of our flock.

But perhaps most importantly, implementing effective ventilation systems is about more than just ensuring the comfort of our chickens—it's about stewardship, and the responsibility we have to care for the creatures entrusted to our care. As we tend to our coops with diligence and care, we're reminded of the interconnectedness of all living things, and the importance of creating spaces where animals can live in harmony with nature.

So let us continue to prioritize proper ventilation in the design and maintenance of our chicken coops, with open hearts and a steadfast commitment to the health and happiness of our feathered friends. And as we watch them roam and roost in their well-ventilated home, surrounded by the gentle breeze and the sounds of contented clucks, let us be reminded of the profound impact we can have when we work in harmony with the natural world.

Designing Practical Nesting Boxes

Nesting boxes are the heart of any chicken coop, providing a cozy and secure space for hens to lay their eggs. As we set out to design practical nesting boxes, we're driven by a desire to create a space that is comfortable, convenient, and conducive to the natural instincts of our feathered friends.

Practicality is key when it comes to designing nesting boxes, and we carefully consider factors such as size, accessibility, and placement. We ensure that the boxes are spacious enough to accommodate multiple hens at once, with plenty of room for them to move around and find a comfortable spot to lay their eggs. We also make sure that the boxes are easy to access for both chickens and humans, with hinged lids or removable panels that allow for quick and convenient egg collection.

But it's not just about functionality—it's also about creating a space that feels safe and inviting for our hens. We line the nesting boxes with soft bedding materials like straw or wood shavings, providing a cozy and comfortable environment for them to nestle into. We also place the boxes in quiet, secluded corners of the coop, away from the hustle and bustle of daily life, to give our hens a sense of privacy and security.

There's a sense of satisfaction that comes from watching our hens use the nesting boxes we've designed, from seeing them settle in and make themselves at home. With each egg laid and each cluck of contentment, we're reminded of the importance of creating a space that meets the needs of our flock and allows them to express their natural behaviors.

But perhaps most importantly, designing practical nesting boxes is about more than just providing a place for our hens to lay their eggs—it's about fostering a deeper connection with the natural world and the creatures that inhabit it. As we observe our hens interact with their nesting boxes, we're reminded of the wonder and beauty of nature, and the role we play in caring for and stewarding the earth and its inhabitants.

So let us continue to design practical nesting boxes with open hearts and a keen eye for detail, ensuring that our hens have a safe and comfortable place to lay their eggs. And as we watch them enjoy the fruits of our labor, let us be reminded of the joy and fulfillment that comes from creating spaces that nurture and support the lives of all creatures, great and small.

Ensuring Predator-Proofing Techniques

In the world of backyard chicken keeping, protecting our feathered friends from predators is of utmost importance. As we set out to ensure predator-proofing techniques, we're driven by a deep sense of responsibility to keep our chickens safe from harm and to provide them with a secure environment to thrive in.

Predators come in all shapes and sizes, from cunning foxes and sly raccoons to crafty coyotes and determined rats. To safeguard our chickens against these threats, we employ a variety of predator-proofing techniques, starting with the design and construction of our coop and run.

We carefully inspect every inch of our coop and run, reinforcing weak spots and fortifying defenses against potential intruders. We use sturdy materials like hardware cloth or welded wire mesh to create a barrier that predators cannot penetrate, ensuring that our chickens are safe and secure inside their enclosure.

But predator-proofing isn't just about physical barriers—it's also about being vigilant and proactive in deterring potential threats. We install motion-activated lights and alarms to scare off nocturnal predators, and we use scent deterrents like predator urine or ammonia to repel curious intruders.

We also employ strategic landscaping techniques, such as planting thorny bushes or dense shrubbery around the perimeter of our coop and run to create a natural barrier that predators are reluctant to cross. And we make sure to keep our coop and run clean and free of food scraps, which can attract unwanted attention from hungry predators.

There's a sense of peace that comes from knowing that we've done everything in our power to protect our chickens from harm. With each predator-proofing measure we implement, we're reminded of the deep bond we share with our feathered friends and the responsibility we have to keep them safe.

But perhaps most importantly, ensuring predator-proofing techniques is about more than just protecting our chickens—it's about honoring the natural order and the delicate balance of life in our backyard ecosystems. As we work to keep predators at bay, we're reminded of the interconnectedness of all living things and the importance of living in harmony with the creatures that share our world.

So let us continue to employ predator-proofing techniques with diligence and care, with open hearts and a steadfast commitment to the safety and well-being of our chickens. And as we watch them scratch and peck in their secure enclosure, surrounded by the sounds of contented clucks and rustling leaves, let us be reminded of the privilege it is to be their guardians and protectors.

Conclusion

Fostering Connection & Community through Backyard Chicken Keeping

In the bustling world we live in, where technology often dominates our interactions and nature can feel distant, backyard chicken keeping offers a unique opportunity to foster connection and community. Through the simple act of caring for our feathered friends, we not only enrich our own lives but also create bonds that transcend fences and property lines.

Backyard chicken keeping has a way of bringing people together, whether it's through sharing tips and advice with fellow chicken enthusiasts, swapping stories of triumphs and challenges, or even just admiring each other's flocks over the fence. It's a reminder that no matter our differences, we all share a common bond as caretakers of these remarkable creatures.

But the connections forged through backyard chicken keeping extend beyond just human relationships—they also encompass the broader community of living beings that inhabit our neighborhoods and ecosystems. As we tend to our chickens and create habitats that support their well-being, we also create havens for other wildlife, from songbirds and butterflies to bees and beneficial insects.

At its core, backyard chicken keeping is about more than just raising chickens—it's about nurturing a sense of connection and belonging, both to each other and to the natural world around us. It's about recognizing our place within the web of life and embracing our role as stewards of the earth and its inhabitants.

As we watch our chickens scratch and peck in the sunshine, surrounded by the sounds of nature and the laughter of children, let us be reminded of the joy and fulfillment that comes from fostering connection and community through backyard chicken keeping. And let us continue to nurture these bonds, knowing that in doing so, we not only enrich our own lives but also contribute to the greater good of our communities and the planet as a whole.

15 Days Tracker

TRACKER

Dates

	MORNING	AFTERNOON	EVENING
MON			
TUE			
WED			
THU			
FRI			
SAT			
SUN			

NOTE:

TRACKER

Dates ___________________

	MORNING	AFTERNOON	EVENING
MON			
TUE			
WED			
THU			
FRI			
SAT			
SUN			

NOTE:

TRACKER

Dates _______________

	MORNING	AFTERNOON	EVENING
MON			
TUE			
WED			
THU			
FRI			
SAT			
SUN			

NOTE:

TRACKER

Dates ______________________

	MORNING	AFTERNOON	EVENING
MON			
TUE			
WED			
THU			
FRI			
SAT			
SUN			

NOTE:

___________________ ___________________ ___________________
___________________ ___________________ ___________________
___________________ ___________________ ___________________
___________________ ___________________ ___________________
___________________ ___________________ ___________________
___________________ ___________________ ___________________

TRACKER

Dates _______________

	MORNING	AFTERNOON	EVENING
MON			
TUE			
WED			
THU			
FRI			
SAT			
SUN			

NOTE:
_______________   _______________   _______________
_______________   _______________   _______________
_______________   _______________   _______________
_______________   _______________   _______________
_______________   _______________   _______________

TRACKER

Dates ______________

	MORNING	AFTERNOON	EVENING
MON			
TUE			
WED			
THU			
FRI			
SAT			
SUN			

NOTE:

_________________ _________________ _________________
_________________ _________________ _________________
_________________ _________________ _________________
_________________ _________________ _________________
_________________ _________________ _________________
_________________ _________________ _________________

TRACKER

Dates _______________

	MORNING	AFTERNOON	EVENING
MON			
TUE			
WED			
THU			
FRI			
SAT			
SUN			

NOTE:

_______________ _______________ _______________
_______________ _______________ _______________
_______________ _______________ _______________
_______________ _______________ _______________
_______________ _______________ _______________
_______________ _______________ _______________

TRACKER

Dates ___________

	MORNING	AFTERNOON	EVENING
MON			
TUE			
WED			
THU			
FRI			
SAT			
SUN			

NOTE:

TRACKER

Dates _______________

	MORNING	AFTERNOON	EVENING
MON			
TUE			
WED			
THU			
FRI			
SAT			
SUN			

NOTE:
____
____
____
____
____
____

TRACKER

Dates
____

	MORNING	AFTERNOON	EVENING
MON			
TUE			
WED			
THU			
FRI			
SAT			
SUN			

NOTE:

_______________ _______________ _______________
_______________ _______________ _______________
_______________ _______________ _______________
_______________ _______________ _______________
_______________ _______________ _______________

TRACKER

Dates ______________________

	MORNING	AFTERNOON	EVENING
MON			
TUE			
WED			
THU			
FRI			
SAT			
SUN			

NOTE:

TRACKER

Dates _______________

	MORNING	AFTERNOON	EVENING
MON			
TUE			
WED			
THU			
FRI			
SAT			
SUN			

NOTE:

TRACKER

Dates ______________

	MORNING	AFTERNOON	EVENING
MON			
TUE			
WED			
THU			
FRI			
SAT			
SUN			

NOTE:

_______________________ _______________________ _______________________
_______________________ _______________________ _______________________
_______________________ _______________________ _______________________
_______________________ _______________________ _______________________
_______________________ _______________________ _______________________

TRACKER

Dates ______________________

	MORNING	AFTERNOON	EVENING
MON			
TUE			
WED			
THU			
FRI			
SAT			
SUN			

NOTE:

______________________ ______________________ ______________________
______________________ ______________________ ______________________
______________________ ______________________ ______________________
______________________ ______________________ ______________________
______________________ ______________________ ______________________

TRACKER

Dates ___________________

	MORNING	AFTERNOON	EVENING
MON			
TUE			
WED			
THU			
FRI			
SAT			
SUN			

NOTE:

_______________ _______________ _______________
_______________ _______________ _______________
_______________ _______________ _______________
_______________ _______________ _______________
_______________ _______________ _______________